Love you always!

– Am~ la

Sorry I didn't talk to you much this year I ~ will ~ though

I will miss you so much. Stay in touch!
– Hamlet

RMA: Macey Jones

I'll miss you

It was wonderful having you as my lab partner for chemistry this year. Please stay away from all bunson burners in the future though.

Thank you for being such a good friend!
RMA

Good luck in all your endeavors
RMA
– Gail

Don't get too wild without me!!

Much Love!

Better Luck Next Year
-RMA ♡ your skipping
Buddy Bob

NO Matder
how high you
climb you can
always climb higher

GOOD LUCK
IN LIFE
-Daniel

Enjoy your summer
- RMA!!!

P.S. You were always the nicest!

I'm going to
miss youry face sooooo
much. Don't forget about
me. Love you lots.
- Tracy

Remember
art class

RMA

RMA

John Yamrus

First edition. Printed in the USA.

Exterior, Cover Page and Chapter Headings by Mish
https://mishmurphy.com/

ISBN: 978-1-926860-65-7

Epic Rites Press publications are distributed worldwide
by Tree Killer Ink. For more information
about *RMA* (and other books and publications from Epic
Rites Press) please visit the Epic Rites website
at www.epicrites.org.

Epic Rites: any press is only as "small" as its thinking

For Kathy

one

i was the loneliest person i ever knew.

i can still hear the way my mother screamed that morning in 1965 when she found my father sitting up, dead in my bed. MY BED...think about that for a minute. my father was dead in my bed and i think i was sleeping on the couch and she screamed not like they do in the movies...not like Fay Wray in King Kong or anything like that, but a scream that was little more than a squeak, but a scream nonetheless, and she ran out into the street still screaming even before i was able to run into that room where i found my father sitting up, blue in the face, eyes open with spit dribbling down his chin...dead, with my past now set in stone and my future laid out before me.

at his best...at his youngest (granted, he was only 45 when he died and as i sit here writing this, i'm an already ancient 67 with all the attendant aches and pains)...at his youngest, he was a very handsome man—or, so i liked to think, and so i was told by many of the people who showed up at his funeral, which was packed from beginning to end and which gave me some odd sort of pride in the fact that if nothing else worked out in his life, at least his funeral was a big success—and, like i said, when he was young, he was handsome, with a broad flat nose that always reminded me of Sugar Ray Robinson, not that he was ever a fighter or anything that i knew of, and he certainly didn't have the moves of The Champ...in fact, come to think of it, my father had a way of walking that maybe was what first made me think of him and Sugar Ray in the same sentence...like a fighter. my father didn't walk or amble or shamble...he kinda *glided,* which was probably very attractive to the ladies when he was young or maybe even not so young, as it showed an assurance and confidence that hinted at a whole lot more.

it's hard to give it the proper words, but think of the way a baseball pitcher walks to the mound...not how he walks *away* from the mound after giving up a home run in the bottom of the ninth to lose the game...no, think of how every pitcher that ever was (if he was any good) walks to the mound, slow and sure...confident in himself and what he can do. Gary Cooper in HIGH NOON, that's how my dad walked.

you reach a point in your life—everyone does, but
especially a writer—where the sound of your own voice
grates on the ear, like fingernails on a blackboard or bad
jazz.

i'm as much a child of the 60s as i am of the decade that
came just before that. the decade in which i was born. the
50s. just ten years, and whole worlds apart.

a good example is me and my sister. just four years
separated us, but it felt then (and still feels) like we're
from two different generations. she's very definitely of
the 50s, while i'm (at least i like to think i am) more
Janis and Jimi. as a kid i drew more from Morrison, the
Beatles, and Dylan the king, than Buddy Holly or even
Elvis, that soon to be drug-addled, fat, and way out of
touch with the times pretender to the throne who called
himself The King. if you asked me...if you looked back
at those times, there's more of the King of Rock and Roll
in Jerry Lee Lewis and that remarkable left hand of his
than Elvis ever had, and Lewis held onto that style and
rock and roll attitude right up until this very day, where i
sit here, writing this on this cloudy rainy morning...

but, i digress...and how's THAT for a nice, writerly word? digress. still, when it comes right down to it, isn't that what a book like this is supposed to be all about? a literary look back?

but, even that's wrong...in an effort to be 100% correct and true and right, i looked it up; *digress* means to deviate from a certain course of action. isn't that what i've pretty much always done my entire life? whether it's looking back at the past or to the left or right. i've never taken a path that took me plain old straight ahead. that's often caused me a lot of trouble, and certainly never made me a lot of money, but, like good jazz, or a conversation between old friends over drinks, my life has never ever gone from point A to point B and then to C...i've always tried to be open. and flexible. that fits in with me being a child of the 60s...flower power. peace love dove and all that other crap.

let it be known that i don't believe in much of anything...certainly not in any kind of organized religion. i've always felt uncomfortable with religion...i've certainly respected the trappings...but, who wouldn't? all that pomp and show and glitz? the church or religion or religion of any kind has served as our rock stars before there WERE rock stars...who wouldn't wet their pants in holy glee seeing the high priest standing at the top of hundreds of stone steps holding up for everyone to see in his bloody hands the still warm and maybe still beating heart of some poor schlubb who just gave it up on the altar of his high appointed lord!

as a kid i was an altar boy and i always felt a certain awe when it came time during the mass to ring the bells, although it was often just a big competition between us altar boys to see who could ring the bells the loudest and the longest, and it was on more than one occasion that i can remember the priest turning around and giving us a look as if to say he'd had enough already and please stop ringing them god-damn bells and would you please get up off your knees and move to the side of the altar and pour that water and wine into my chalice and go very easy on the water and heavy on the wine, if you know what's good for you.

that's about the full extent of MY religion.

but, as fleeting as that contact was, it still had its effect on me.

it was all around me. it was everywhere.

like the church steeple in Proust's town of Combray, if i stood in my back yard i could see the grey slate roof and gold painted cross of St. John's church where we went on Sundays. i could hear the bells ringing for mass or funerals. i could even hear the bells from the other churches in the neighborhood—and there were tons of them—churches all over the place. maybe as many churches as there were bars.

and each church, like each bar, had its own crowd of regulars...its own tone and feel, right down to the sound of the bells.

for example...the church out near Luzerne, maybe six blocks from us, didn't really have bells...it had a recording that rang out every Sunday, which was really new and unusual for back then...those bells had a thin, high pitched sound.

i guess every writer at one point or another comes up with a book like this (this is my 2nd)...a look back over the shoulder. some are true. some aren't. i'll try to make this one as true as i can, without resorting to making something up, which would make it a lie, then, wouldn't it?

anyway, back to those bells...the ones at St. Mary's church, which was a few blocks from our back yard...that was the church that seemed to compete with the one i went to with my family. that one was St. John's. i was an altar boy there. skinny, short, and bowlegged. with hair that was often still wet from standing at the kitchen sink where my mother would run a comb through it and make a part in it, crisp and clear and sharp. and wet. i can still feel the cool wet of that water as it sank into my scalp and dribbled down the back of my neck.

Three

have you ever read THE BIG SEA by Langston Hughes?
it's an incredible book. with simple, wonderful words.
it's got lines equal to the best of Mark Twain and Ernest
Hemingway. Effortless stuff. it's the kind of book that
makes me wish i had a chance to read it when i was 15
or so and just starting to discover writers like Kerouac
and Nelson Algren and even James Jones.

i wonder what my 15 year-old heart would have made of
it? THE BIG SEA. how would it have moved me? i can
picture myself walking back and forth in the back yard
as i often did back then in the summer, reading
Kerouac's THE SUBTERRANEANS out loud, not
caring who was watching me from their windows or
yard, maybe even hoping just a little that someone
actually *was*...that they *did* see this crazy, skinny kid
with the bad, wet hair, walking back and forth on the
grass. would Hughes have had that sort of seismic effect
on me? maybe he wouldn't. his writing lacked the sort of
wild abandon that Kerouac (at his best) had...that prose
that felt like poetry...prose that exploded my head...so
much so that i was pretty much convinced that the
neighbors, watching me pace back and forth in the yard,
with my still wet head, sometimes even with tears in my

eyes, reading Kerouac...that they'd see me with my skull split clean wide open and my brains splattered all over the green, wet grass of the small back yard.

the same yard that up until the time i was 15 or so, or maybe even later, had a little garden in the back right corner...five or six or seven rows of mostly tomatoes, with every now and then potatoes, and i think i even remember cabbage that my father used to dust with this white powder to keep away the bugs. i used to hate having to hook up the hose and drag it across the yard to water those things.

we also had a set of swings in the yard. i think they were red.

somewhere along the line over the course of my life i'm sure i've been asked over and over again, "who or what in the world do you love more than anybody or anything?" as with anyone, that answer has changed with time...morphed into something that i don't even recognize anymore. but, back then, if anyone had asked me that question, without a doubt i would have answered "that yard." it, more than anything else, felt like home to me.

the inside of our house certainly wasn't home.

it was too poor...too spare...certainly, not like any of the houses i'd seen in the movies.

there were no polished floors, no butlers, no tinkling, jingling glasses and jewels. just a plain old house with grey peeling siding. a house that smelled of cabbage and potatoes and onions, and in the summer, smelled of the honeysuckle that grew in yellow abundance on the right hand side of the front porch.

the porch was a sort of battleship grey.

my mother painted it the summer after my father died.

the front railing was white and ran around two sides of the porch. the honeysuckle was on the right and the steps were on the left. the steps looked out at the garage that served as a shed for the neighbors we never liked. an old man and his two spinster daughters. all three of them were crazy.

the one daughter never spoke.

she was short and fat and always wore an apron over her dress, which was always wrinkled and dirty and came down to her ankles, which were also wrinkled and dirty. she had shoes like my grandmother.

the father every now and then would walk out the back door (which faced our back yard) and talk to the "girls" in Polish or Lithuanian or Slovak or something. i could never make it out as he always mumbled, and i never understood the words, anyway, so it didn't really matter.

the other daughter—the youngest of the three—would talk to their cats.

she had a bowl for them that she kept on the top step of their back porch. their back porch and back steps (like ours) were also grey, but there was a certain sadness about them (if steps and a porch can be said to be sad). they were spooky, too...mostly because they led into that house...a great big white fearful house that was only two floors, but felt much higher and taller, so much so that it seemed to tower menacingly over ours, looking into our yard, keeping an eye on everything we said or did or thought or felt.

i hadn't read THE HOUSE OF THE SEVEN GABLES back then, but, years later, when i first encountered that book and saw that title, this great big horrible house was the first image that came to mind.

it didn't look anything like Hawthorne's famous house, but i was totally convinced (and maybe to a little bit still am) that its halls were crammed with ghosts, dead things, and the stuff that makes for nightmares in the night.

the old man was maybe the creepiest and scariest of all.

i have no idea how old he was and, even now, can't imagine his age, and it's wrong for me to even try and figure it out. he was ageless. ancient. numberless. always bent, in dirty filthy clothes...long, grey hair that was never combed, and i'm sure that he smelled. not of dirt or sweat or anything like that...but of the grave...of ghosts and death and the kind of horrors only kids can dream.

did i mention that they fenced their property with barbed wire?

they had what seemed like a lot of land for the neighborhood.

besides their large, dilapidated house and their garage that never held a car...only secrets, darkness, and ghosts as far as i could tell...they had a huge garden area that took up the entire corner of the block.

it had no plan to it that i could see...just random groups of roses, berries, tomatoes, flowers, and weeds. for the old man to walk between them he had to push things aside and sometimes walk sideways and even raise his arms into the air. it was a wildman's yard, and, like i said, it was bordered by a fence made up of three terrible lines of barbed wire laid close to the sidewalk, so close that you had to be careful when you rode by on your bike, and you never rode past it two by two for fear of scraping up against it and ripping your arms and legs bloody.

i hated it.
i hated him. and i hated them. and i hated that yard.

if you happened to be playing near there, and had the bad luck to have a ball land in their yard, forget about it...it was gone forever.

the second a ball went over the fence, like magic, one of those women would open the back door, run down the grey painted steps, and grab the ball and take it away. gone. forever.

they must have been watching us...standing on that back porch of theirs, looking out from behind the curtains.

in those few times that i can remember when a ball went into the yard and they *didn't* come running right out— (those women—those crazies—those screaming, addled, wacky crones) —we'd muster up whatever courage we had in our 9 year-old hearts and run like hell into the yard, ignoring the barbed wire, the ruts, and the bushes and the stones and grab the ball and run back, convinced those harpies were either running down the stairs after us or flying across the yard on hellish witches' wings.

if we made it back safely across the line, the border between life and death, we smiled and laughed and ran like hell all the way down the street.

hell actually figured deep in the images we had of that house. it was everything we learned to fear...and more.

it was a great big malevolent gray haired screaming god.

across the street...on the same side of the road as us, but across the street and facing the house of horrors, also on the corner, was a bar owned by the uncle of the political aide who was drowned in Chappaquiddick, in that mess that derailed Ted Kennedy's presidential bid.

the bar was owned by a man named John and his wife. actually, i think the wife owned it. they bought it from her father, a kindly, white-haired old man who always sat in the bar on the first stool just inside the door.

John played the drums.

no one ever called him John.

not his friends. not us kids. not his wife. no one.

to everyone who knew him he was just Gumpy. it wasn't even until a good many years later, when i was grown and married, that i came back to town for a funeral or something, that i saw that the sign out front didn't say Gumpy's...that the window near the door didn't read Gumpy's.

the bar was long since closed. the place was shut down. even the sign out front (it was a neon arrow of some sort) was gone. i can't remember what it used to read, but i'm sure it didn't say Gumpy's, but that didn't matter.

as for The Gump himself, he used to sit on a stool behind the bar...just inside the front window, where the evening sun would shine through and warm his back. every now and then he'd get up, pour himself a shot, and sit back down. i can't say i ever saw him drunk...or maybe it was that i never saw him sober.

also, many years later...just recently, in fact, a very long time after Gumpy was dead, i was watching a documentary on the Kennedys and they were doing a spot on Teddy and Chappaquiddick and they showed the funeral for Mary Jo...and there, standing at the grave among the crowd, right next to Ted, elbow to elbow, in a nice new suit, was Gumpy.

but, that was much later...at the time i'm thinking of...the time that firmly and permanently *fixed* Gumpy in my memory is maybe the late 50s or early 60s...a time of watching Mort Sahl on The Ed Sullivan Show (i was too young to appreciate the cerebral, groundbreaking Sahl and didn't think him funny at all, not anything like Abbott and Costello or The Stooges or even Red Skelton)...and Buddy Holly and Elvis, although i can't remember ever really liking Elvis, either, and my first real memory of *him* is me being in my kitchen on a

Sunday morning, listening to that little brown radio we kept on the table between the front door and the front kitchen window.

above the radio was a cheap framed copy of an illustration of a very handsome white man, Jesus knocking on some wooden door (my mother used to drill it into me—that was Jesus knocking on the door to my heart. i hated that). i hated Jesus. i hated everything about the man.

he had no right to be knocking at the door to my heart or knocking anywhere for that matter...and the same went for Elvis, but he had a lot more power at the time than Jesus, even though that song he had about the hound dog was just plain flat out stupid. in my book, he couldn't hold a candle to Buddy Holly or Gene Vincent or Little Richard or Chuck Berry or even Ritchie Valens. now, THEY had power...and Jesus was just some guy in a cheap Woolworth calendar print banging on a door and it didn't mean a single thing to me.

speaking of prints...
and Gumpy...and that bar of his...at the far end of the
bar, in the main room, on the wall at the right (just
outside the phone booth sized bathroom that was for both
men and women...on the wall was another cheap print,
but a whole lot cooler than the one on the wall at home...

it was a patriotic stylized print of Custer's Last Stand,
complete with blood-thirsty crowds of fired-up Indians,
surrounding the last few living members of Custer's
doomed command...with bodies and blood
everywhere...jumping horses, dying men...bullets,
arrows, and still more blood, and there in the middle of it
all, wounded, bloodied, but still unbowed, the yellow
haired embodiment of Invictus...the heroic George
Armstrong Custer, standing with one foot atop a rock,
holding a pistol in his hand, aimed at a wildly charging
mass of Indians intent on taking his scalp and leaving
him dead like all the rest.

the boy in me loved that print, and i think i looked at it
every single time i went in the place.

through a door at the back of the bar was the kitchen where the family lived. actually, there was no door there that i can remember...just a curtain. a dark red curtain.

and through the doorway you could see the kitchen table and smell whatever it was that they were cooking for dinner. i never saw them eat, but i still remember the smells.

behind the bar, in another room that faced the street, was the "banquet room"...it was just another room, no bigger or smaller than the bar, with a few tables and chairs and a dart board, and one of those coin operated bowling games that was kinda like shuffleboard.

the tables were cheap, dark brown wood, and the place smelled of smoke, spilled beer and grime.

the only entrance to the room was the large opening that came from the bar, and the only window was small and quite high off the floor. it was colored stained glass. i don't remember what it said.

due to local "blue" laws, which prevented liquor sales on Sunday, the place was supposed to only be open six days a week, but on any given Sunday, if you were a regular (and regulars were the only ones who ever came to the place), you could walk to the back door, bang on the window, and the curtains would soon be pulled aside and a face would look out (usually Gumpy's wife, a thin,

woman with dark dyed hair who always wore an apron)
and you'd be let in through the kitchen into the bar...past
whatever was cooking on the stove.

i can't remember if they ever had a dog.

there's a scene in THE BIG SEA in which Langston
Hughes describes getting a job as crew on a freighter in
the 1920s, heading toward Africa.

for company on the trip, he had taken with him a box of
books.

shortly after setting sail from New York, he looked at the
books and (i guess as a symbol of leaving something
behind), one by one, he threw the books overboard off
the back of the ship.

he said it was like throwing a million bricks out of his
heart.

i know how he felt.

i know the feeling of carrying a great unshakeable
weight inside you year after year. mine was never the
same weight that Hughes had with him. it's not the same
weight as YOU may have.

it's mine and i'm happy for it.

i don't think i can ever do what Hughes did and throw mine overboard. i'm too selfish for that. i like taking my pain (or whatever that weight is) out of its box every now and then and examining it. getting a closer look for myself and locking it back up again.

seven

now, moving on up the street...past Gumpy's, heading away from our house, there was a large open field to the right (across the street from the bar) which was part of a property owned by a man and his wife and their daughters. i don't remember if there were two or three girls...and it doesn't matter...at least not for me...at least not for this story. nor does it matter that their field (the part of the property that sat right on the corner, where there could have stood another house)...their field was filled with old cars in various stages of repair.

today i was reading this book about Bob Dylan, and in it someone said that his songs take him "out to the meadow"...in my mind, that's the meadow i picture...that corner lot filled with junk and gravel and cars...that lot where a house could have been built. that lot with a gravel drive right down the middle.

that's my meadow.

or, maybe it's the *other* meadow...the one just a block down the street from there...toward the tracks...a more or less *actual* meadow (as i knew them back then, with unmowed grass that came up over your ankles and dirtied your pants).

the meadow stood at the top of a slope that ran down to a deeper cut in that valley where we all lived...the part of the valley that eventually flooded badly in the hurricane called Agnes in 1972.

a couple of times one summer, i would fly a kite down there...in that meadow.

it was a yellow kite with torn strips of rag for a tail. only once did i manage to get it up to any real height. most of the time, i ran back and forth through the grass at the top of the hill. usually giving up, walking back home, tired and discouraged.

but, there was one time i really DID get it to fly, and man, that still sticks in my head.

i remember that once it got up into the wind and started taking off on its own, i didn't really have to run anymore...i just stood there (more or less), trying to keep the line tight, just playing out enough string, hand over hand, to let it go higher and higher and higher, until it was nearly out of sight...a wonderful, exhilarating little blot of yellow way up there in the sky, threatening to reach the clouds, which were white and high, splashed across the blue…that still stays with me in my mind.

getting back now to that religious thing...maybe it was an exaggeration to say i hated Jesus...but, i certainly wasn't any kind of a fan. even more so than most of the kids my age. but, unlike the others, who probably deep down felt that they'd eventually fall in line, i was always skeptical of what i was taught...and much of what i was taught was *so* misguided, one-sided, stupid, hateful and wrong, that it couldn't help BUT make me less than enthusiastic about the religion i grew up with. the religion that pervaded the valley where i lived...that hung over our lives like a great, dark overpowering cloud.

the best example i can give (and i can give many) is a teacher i had in one of my early grades...a nun, who was asked a question about one of the religions...i don't remember what religion it was (exactly), if i ever knew, but i DO remember it was in a class where we were learning about different countries and the people in them. and let me back up here a bit...remember that this was a coal mining community...a church school that i went to...a school that taught us Slovak and was taught by nuns with regular visits from one of the two church priests on a weekly basis. the school and the whole community was insulated...almost cut off (in a way) from the rest of the world, in the sense that we were Polish and Slovak and Lithuanian kids, and that's all we knew.

even knowing a Jew back then was a big deal and really exotic and rare...and don't even think about a person of color...they were only on TV and lived in big cities, and we learned about them only when we talked about the Civil War—which we talked about a lot, as this was the 100th anniversary of that war between brothers and the local paper would run weekly "updates" on what was going on that week in history 100 years before and i looked forward each week to the battles and maneuvers that were described and i waited what felt like years and years for the week the paper would run the battle of Gettysburg, which to me was the ultimate and best and neatest battle ever.

so, in talking about India in that class way back then, one of the kids in the class (it might even have been me for all i know...and i don't...it was so very long ago)...asked why's *their* religion isn't the real one? and the nun looked shocked to be even asked such a stupid, foolish question, and she stood there in her black and white habit...ironed, pressed and starched and stiff...and she said, as clear as any memory i have from then, "because *they* don't value life the way we do...in their religion, they think that whatever happens is god's will and there's just no changing it and if they're doing something like riding in a boat and someone falls overboard, they'll

just sit there and watch while that person drowns right in
front of them, even if it's their son or daughter or mother
or father...they think that's just the way their god
intended it and they just don't care."

how's *that* for making you think about things? how's
that for turning you against nuns and Jesus and a religion
that had so much hate built into it that it had no room at
all for any ideas other than its own?

according to what i was taught back then, Martin Luther
was (at best) an abomination, worth only mentioning in
whispers. in school, independent thought was never
encouraged. Friedrich Nietzsche was as close to the devil
as you could imagine. just mention the name Nietzsche,
and you were given frozen stares and considered to be
more than halfway crazy.

thinking myself to be happily more than half-way crazy,
i tried reading Nietzsche back then, but found myself
quickly bored out of my happily halfway crazy brain.

i failed to see just what the fuss was all about.

now, getting back to that neighborhood and that street...

if you stood on my front porch and looked to the left,
you'd see that garage and house next door where the
madman and his two daughters lived.

across the street from there was the bar and across the
street from that, was the field with the cars and that great
big house.

it was grey.

looking further up the street...up a very slight incline,
were a set of railroad tracks that crossed the road. just
before you got to the tracks, on the right, was the squat
green house where my friend Willie lived. Willie was
gay. i didn't know it then...none of us did...with the
possible exception of Willie himself, but maybe back
then not even he did, because we were all just kids and
young and trying to figure everything out.

i didn't know very much about Willie, except that he was
my friend.

Willie was different from all my other friends.

he didn't play football with us. he didn't play baseball. he never played basketball. i only knew that Willie used to do really interesting things. he liked to draw. he liked to lay out in the grass near the tracks and look up at the clouds...and talk.

Willie really liked to talk.

Willie could talk for hours, laying there in the warm weeds near the tracks. i liked Willie.

fifty years later i ran into him on the street on one of my rare trips back "home." he was bald and bent and walked really slow. he reminded me a lot of his mother, who i knew back when Willie and i both walked a whole lot faster.

i never knew his father, who must have died or ran off before i knew Willie. if i had to guess, i'd say he probably ran off or at least wished himself into an early grave because Willie's mother was a real pain in the ass, and i hated every minute i had to spend in the same room with her. she, just like Willie, even when i was a kid, seemed old and bent.

she was nasty and shouted and screamed.

i knew she didn't like me. when i was around her, i felt dirty and cheap and poor. and all she was, was nasty and old and bent.

just beyond their kitchen, in the TV room, at Christmas
time, they used to put up a huge six foot aluminum
tree...silver. with silver balls and silver garland.
aluminum trees were big then. for a couple of years
everyone who could afford one had an aluminum tree.

we never did.

but, Willie and his mother and father and his two sisters
who were always out of the house sure as shootin' did.

for a time, one of the daughters went off and became a
nun. eventually, she left the convent nunnery or
nunhood, or whatever it is you call it, and got married.

i never knew her.

the other sister was four or five years older than me. i
never knew her, either.

one of the two sisters was tall and thin. the other was tall
and not.

i never knew either.

eleven

Willie had the basement all to himself. he did have a small bedroom just off the TV room, at the back of the house. in it, there was a desk and a closet and eventually, the wall was covered with some of the paintings that he did, which were not very good. and some of the photos he took, which were also not very good. but he was just a kid and just starting to feel his way around the world in which he was meant to live.

that little room just off the TV room, where they had the silver tree at Christmas, which was just off the kitchen where his mother would sit at the table all day, just sitting and staring out the window at the road...it was just the room where he slept. it didn't mean a thing to him.

he seemed to spend most of his time down in the basement, which was one great big room as large as the house.

except for the washer and a clothes line that ran the full length of the room, the entire basement belonged to Willie. it was where he lived. where he read and where he ate. where he tried his hand at painting and photography.

like i said, Willie was a talker.

he liked to talk. i think he liked the way he sounded
when he talked. like most people who like to talk and
like the sound of the way they talk, he talked really
slow...like every word he said had weight and meaning.
if you tried to say something...some idea of your own, or
if you made the great mistake of interrupting him, he'd
stop talking and just look at you.

he'd just sit and stare...and wait. and when you finally
got the idea and shut up, he'd start all over again. from
the very beginning.

just talking.

that was Willie.

if you continued up the street...all the way to the final corner at the end of the final block (understand that the street was only five blocks long...two to the right of my house, and three to the left. five short blocks), the street i lived on came to an end...a T that crossed itself at Main Street, which wasn't any real kind of a main street as most of us think of Main Streets anywhere at any time. this Main Street wasn't even centrally located in town, but actually ran around the perimeter of one part of town...and, more improbably, wasn't even known to locals as Main Street, but was referred to by everyone in the area simply as The Back Road.

and if you followed this street, which wasn't much of a street, which didn't have much of a name...if you looked to the left or looked to the right, there wasn't much of anything there to see.

there was the little mom and pop sporting goods store where fishing and hunting licenses were bought, and bullets and guns and fishing lures were sold.

i don't think i was ever in that place more than twice in my entire life.

my father would go there once a year (i guess) for his fishing license, and we never had the money for expensive fancy lures, so we didn't need to buy any of those.

instead, we'd get worms for fishing...late at night in the back yard, with a flashlight, walking really quiet and slow and shining the light kinda not directly on the ground because if it shone directly on a worm that had come up from the dirt into the grass, it would dive right back in and be gone forever.

no, you just used the flashlight obliquely and moved slow enough until you got your hand right above the hopefully unsuspecting worm and then you pounced and grabbed it and if you didn't pull too hard and rip it in half, you put it into your coffee can or tomato can or whatever it was you held that night to carry your growing pile of worms.

when you were done and had what you felt were enough to last through the next day, you pulled some weeds and grass and maybe even a little bit of dirt, sprinkling it lightly with water, put it in the can and capped it up, with holes poked in the top of the cap, and saved it on the porch till morning.

and, if you looked to the right, down that street that wasn't really a street and didn't really have a name, there was a bar that my parents very rarely went to.

the owner was famous around town for having pitched a couple of games in the big leagues...for the Yankees, no less.

i never saw the man in my entire life, but i knew who he was and where he lived and what he was said to have done.

it was quite a big deal. we all loved baseball. we all revered baseball players. we saw the movies about their lives. we bought and collected and traded the cards. and if we had one of our own who had actually made it to the big leagues, no matter for how long or short a time it was...as far as anyone was concerned, that man walked on water.

the bar went broke and closed in the 1980s.

i heard somewhere that someone was writing a book about him and his baseball years.

i never heard anything more.

thirteen

past the bar, with its white fluorescent sign hung above the sidewalk, a white arrow, outlined in red neon. the arrow had the name of the bar on it in script. the name of that now dead ballplayer was written on it. the arrow pointed in, away from the street...and down, towards the door.

if you walked past that door and down that street, you'd have the laundromat on the right, with its large glass windows looking in.

all it was, was one great big room, bigger even than Willie's basement, a room with washers on one side and dryers on the other, with a large wooden folding table running down the middle.

when money was tight (tighter than i care to think or tell) and our washer was broke, my mother and i used to carry huge trash bags of clothes up the street from our house...up the block. across the tracks. past the bar.

and we'd spend an hour or two getting things done...washed and dried and folded and bagged. walking back again, past the bar and across the tracks.

home.

it was always home.

home with the grey front porch with the white trim.

home, with the cheap grey siding. home, with the back yard with the swing and the garden that needed picking and planting and watering in the summer when the sky was warm and high and new.

fourteen

there were very few paved sidewalks along the back road.

there was also a lot of traffic for such a small town, which made walking it a little dangerous. it was even more so if you were riding a bike, which we all did back then. but there was one summer when, for some long-forgotten reason, my bike was out of commission, and i regularly rode the handlebars of my all-time, written in stone best friend Lenny.

a year younger than me, Lenny was a big guy, my exact mirror opposite.

where i was short and skinny, with bow legs and zero body fat, Len was huge, somewhat overweight, and was inclined to lumber when he ran.

Lenny was my best friend in the whole wide world.

i think i could have died for him.

once, during that wonderful, incredible summer, me and
Lenny got into a fight with a bunch of kids from
downtown who made the mistake of calling him fat.

it was just me and him—Mutt and Jeff—but we took on
and beat four or five (it seemed like twelve) bigger, older
kids, who didn't know that we had lightning in our hands
and power in our hearts.

that's the way we saw it. we two. me and Len.

anyway, me and Len, we did everything together, and
that included me riding perched up, wild and dangerous
and high on the handlebars of his bike.

we were fearless, there was nothing in the world we
wouldn't do or try...and that included approaching and
attacking *killer hill.*

fifteen

we had names for everything back then.

stupid names. names right out of Tom Sawyer and Huck Finn.

killer hill was just one of many.

to get to killer hill, you just walked past (or, in our case, rode your bike past) the bar and the laundromat, and there it was...

just another small street on another small hill in another small town. but, to us it was *killer hill*...the hill to end all hills. the challenge of all challenges.

we could rattle off all the names (true or not) of all our friends and some of our enemies who had ridden down that hill, pedaling at top speed and summoning up all the courage a nine or ten or even older kid may have and...maybe halfway down the hill, taken their hands off the grips, throwing caution (and their lives) to the wind and for the briefest of times, just FLYING...before they crashed and burned and shake, rattle, and rolled all the way down to a bloody, crying stop.

we knew they cried, even though they swore they never did.

we knew it because we knew that if it ever happened to us, we'd sure as shit cry and maybe even walk home crying, hoping against hope and fate and all the wonders of the world that our mom or someone would be there waiting for us to hold us and say it was going to be all right and maybe even kiss away the tears.

sixteen

so, me and Len...the big guy and his little friend...one day we finally went and did it.

we finally screwed up the courage to take our turn at killer hill.

it wasn't something we talked about or planned...it was just one of those things that seemed to come up and happen.

there we were, one day...a nice, hot, sunshiny summer day...with not a single cloud marking the sky.

we were out riding around on his bike...him at the pedals and me sitting on the handlebars, just riding around, and before we even knew it...there we were...

the two of us on his bike...sitting there...poised...waiting...at the top of killer hill.

seventeen

at the bottom of the hill, if we managed to make it...if we didn't blow a tire or run off the road or run head-on into an oncoming, unseeing car...just two blocks and a lifetime away, at the end of killer hill, was an old gas station on a corner of the road.

just before you got to the gas station (that never sold much gas, but was always more than busy doing body work and oil changes and fixing flats)...just before you got to the gas station, there was a little gravel covered field, which was nothing more than a glorified drive that led to a path that led up another hill that led back to my house.

at the top of that path was an old oak tree that we actually called *the old oak tree.*

there was a wooden hand rail that followed the way of the path up from the bottom of the hill all the way to the railroad tracks at the top.

in the summer, we'd climb the oak tree and sit in the crook of its branches and listen for trains.

in the winter, we rode our sleds down the path all the way to the bottom and past the garage, nearly out into the street.

eighteen

i don't think i'll tell you if me and Lenny actually made it all the way to the bottom of the hill on his bike or if we fell down in a horrific pile somewhere along the way.

i won't tell you because it doesn't matter.

what matters is that we were just two kids...two young kids who loved and trusted one another as only young kids can.

who cared enough to take that hill with all the crazy guts and joy we had.

nineteen

when the old man next door finally gave up and died, my mother was the only one who went to the funeral home.

the daughters were there.

i don't know if they ever even talked.

twenty

near the end of that year...or, at the very least, at some
time during that summer...me and Len were sitting on
the floor in his room, looking through his older sister's
year book. inside the front and back covers, every inch
of it was filled with autographs and little personal
phrases written by each person. at the end of every
inscription, usually below the signature, it often said
"RMA," which was a stupid, silly abbreviation for
"Remember me always."

we laughed and finished the plate of brownies his mother
had made.

. . .

the very next year Len was gone.

his mother and father sold the little grocery store they
owned and moved away.

i heard it might have been New York.

Also by John Yamrus

Memory Lane (memoir)
As Real As Rain
I Admit Nothing
Burn
Endure
Alchemy
Bark
They Never Told Me This Would Happen
Can't Stop Now!
Doing Cartwheels On Doomsday Afternoon
New And Selected Poems
Blue Collar
Shoot The Moon
One Step at a Time
78 RPM
Keep The Change
New And Used
Start To Finish
Someone Else's Dreams (novel)
Something
Poems
Those
Coming Home
American Night
15 Poems
Heartsongs
Lovely Youth (novel)
I Love

Epic Rites Press